THE ANGEL AND THE THREE MEN
Prophet Muhammad for Little Hearts

by
SANIYASNAIN KHAN

Once the Prophet Muhammad ﷺ told his Companions the story of three of the Children of Israel—a leper, a bald man and a blind man. To test the gratitude of these three poor men, Allah sent an angel to each of them.

To the leper, the angel said, "Of all things, which would you most love to have?" The leper replied, "A beautiful complexion, beautiful skin and a cure for the ailment for which people shun me." So the angel passed his hands over the man, and his wishes were granted. The angel again asked, "Of all things, what would you most love to possess?" "Camels," he replied. So he was given a pregnant she-camel. As the angel left, he said, "May Allah bless it."

To the man with the diseased scalp, the angel said, "Of all things, what would you most love to have?" The man replied, "Beautiful hair and a cure for the disease for which people shun me." So the angel passed his hands over him and his wishes were granted. Again the angel asked, "Of all things, what would you most love to possess?" "Cows," he replied. So he was given a pregnant cow. And the angel said, "May Allah bless it."

To the blind man, the angel said, "Of all things, what would you most love to have?" He replied, "My sight restored by Allah, so that I can see people." So the angel passed his hands over him, and he regained his sight. Then the angel said, "Of all things, what would you most love to possess?" "Sheep," he replied. So he was given a ewe with its lambs. And the angel said, "May Allah bless them."

All the animals multiplied, so that the first man had a valley full of camels, the second a valley full of cows and the third a valley full of sheep.

Later, the angel came in the guise of a leper to the first man and said, "I am a poor man, unable to travel any further without Allah's help—or yours. By the One who has given you wealth and a beautiful skin and complexion, give me a camel to ride on my journey."

The man replied, "I have too many obligations." The angel said, "I seem to recognize you. Weren't you once a leper whom people shunned? And weren't you poor before Allah gave you so much?" The man replied, "I inherited this wealth from a nobleman, who inherited it from a nobleman." The angel said, "If you are a liar, may Allah turn you back into a leper."

Then, in the guise of a bald man, he came to the man who had once had a diseased scalp and made the same request as he had to the first man. His plea was similarly turned down. The angel said, "If you are a liar, may Allah turn you back into a bald man."

Coming to the third man in the guise of a blind man, he said, "I am a poor, homeless man, unable to reach my destination, unless Allah, or you, can help me. By the One who restored your sight, give me a ewe to help me on my way."

The man said, "I was blind, and Allah restored my sight. So take whatever you will and leave whatever you will, for, by Allah, I will not grudge you anything you take for His sake."

The angel said, "Keep your wealth, for you were only being tested. You may keep your blessings, but your companions have lost all."

The moral of the story is that we should learn to be thankful to Allah for His blessings. Allah likes our thankfulness and increases His blessings manifold on those who show thankfulness to Him. And those who do not show thankfulness will be in loss as Allah being All-power, will take away His blessings from them. One should know that Allah does not like those who are boastful, arrogant and do not show thankfulness to Him.